Truth or Dare

This Book Belongs To

_____

HOW TO PLAY

Truth or dare... the choice is yours! Things are going to get hot, wild and very sexual either way...

Explore and flirt with your own sexual boundaries, as well as discover more about your partner's boundaries and deepest sexual desires. Tease and play and try new sexual acts whilst feeling out of control during this sexual adventure you are about to embark on...

The pleasure comes from both partners feeling free and playful enough to try new sexual things together and get more intimate sexually. It's not about seeing your partner squirm or feel pressured to do something they wouldn't normally do.

Remember consent is key and "playing" rather then "pushing" is sexy.

1.There is one "truth or dare" scenario on each page. Deicide on either a time limit or question limit for the game.

2.Partner A looks at the page and asks partner B to choose "Truth or dare" without partner B seeing the page. (This adds an extra element of fun to the game as it allows partner B to try to read the body language and facial expressions of their partner when deciding which to pick, whilst partner A has to try to keep a "poker face" as to what they would prefer partner B to choose).

3.Partner B chooses and partner A either asks the question (if partner B chose "Truth") or partner A reads out the dare partner B must now perform (if partner B chose "Dare").

 CONT...

4. Take turns passing the book back and forth. (No looking ahead to the next questions/pages as that will ruin the surprise).

5. If a dare is an action that must be performed in the future then both partners make a note of it AND schedule it in right now so it happens. There is no getting out of it! And it gives you both moments to look forward to and tease each other with as the dates draw near.

6. If a partner selects either "truth or dare" but then won't answer/ do the dare then they have to do the NEXT TWO "truth or dare" scenarios on the next pages.

7. Keep going till you run out of time or reach your question limit.

These naughty questions and dirty dares are designed for you to have fun together, create some amazing sexual memories and to feel more connected and free sexually with each other.

Whether you're dating, are newlyweds or have been married for ages, spice up your sex life and be open to learning new things about your partner and yourself. The fact you're playing this game together shows you're both invested in having a wonderful sex life!
How romantic (AND EXCITING) is that?!

Have fun playing
and exploring!

TRUTH

What one "sexual superpower" do you wish you had?

 **OR**

Whisper in my ear something you've fantasized about while you've made yourself cum.

DARE

TRUTH

What's the most number of times you've had sex in one day?

 **OR**

Pretend you're performing oral sex the way YOU like it by sucking on my finger for 30 seconds.

DARE

TRUTH

What do you think is the
sexiest part of my body?

 **OR**

Let me blindfold and tease
you for 5 minutes any way i
choose.

DARE

TRUTH

What's the most public place you've had sex with someone?

 **OR**

Sext me the dirtiest message you can think of.

DARE

TRUTH

What sex fetish are you
curious to try in real life?

 **OR**

Seductively kiss me and try
to get me to lose control and
kiss you back.

DARE

TRUTH

What's the most exciting sex dream you've ever had?

 **OR**

Get your favorite sex toy and straddle me (if you're a woman)/or kneel in front of me (if you're a man) as you look into my eyes and seductively describe what you like to do with it and how it makes you feel.

DARE

TRUTH

Describe the last time you were so turned on you couldn't stand it and what you were thinking about?

 **OR**

Show me with your hands what you want my tongue to do all over your body for 5 minutes.

DARE

TRUTH

Has the best sex you've had with me been when we've been in love or when you didn't know me so well at the time?

 **OR**

Show me a porn clip you like from a porn website.

DARE

TRUTH

How many sex partners do you believe is "too many"?

 **OR**

Show me the sexiest picture you have of yourself on your phone.

DARE

TRUTH

Would you rather spank me or be spanked?

 **OR**

Put something sweet, soft and gooey you love to eat on my chest and lick it off sexy and slow.

DARE

TRUTH

What's one sexual thing you wish i'd do more?

 **OR**

Let me tie your hands/ handcuff you and i'll do one sex act i know you'll enjoy.

DARE

TRUTH

If you had to pick one BDSM act to do to me what would it be?

 **OR**

Pretend to have the best orgasm of you life right now.

DARE

TRUTH

Who's the most inappropriate person you've had a sexual fantasy about?

 **OR**

Go get me a drink and snacks and serve it to me naked and wearing just an apron.

DARE

TRUTH

If you had to pick a celebrity for us to have a threesome with, who would it be?

 **OR**

Give me a lap dance.

DARE

TRUTH

What's your biggest sexual regret?

 **OR**

Let me tease you by going down on you. I'm going to hum a song and will only make you cum when you can guess what it is.

DARE

TRUTH

How many times a month do you masturbate?

 **OR**

Try to turn me on by touching me without touching any sexual parts for 10 minutes.

DARE

TRUTH

Would you have sex with an ugly stranger for one night and then you never have to see them again for "change your life money"? And if so, what's your number?

 **OR**

Unzip and pull down my trousers/skirt using just your teeth.

DARE

TRUTH

If you could be the best in
the world at one sexual act,
what would it be?

 **OR**

Describe an x-rated version
of our first date.

DARE

TRUTH

What's one thing that gets you really turned on every time that i don't know about?

 **OR**

Have sex with me right now in a position we've never done it before.

DARE

TRUTH

What's your favorite sexual
memory?

 **OR**

Strike the most seductive
pose that you can right now
and hold it for two minutes
as i really take you in.

DARE

TRUTH

If you could experience what it's like having sex in the body of an animal what animal would you choose?

 **OR**

Seductively sing me the chorus of a sexy song that turns you on. (We might giggle nervously but try to "own it" as that is what will turn me even if i act like it doesn't).

DARE

TRUTH

What's the most number of times you've touched yourself in one day?

 **OR**

Let me sketch a picture of you naked.

DARE

TRUTH

Describe the plot of an erotic movie or book that really turned you on.

 **OR**

Let me dress you up in an outfit i find really sexy and wear it for the rest of the game for me.

DARE

TRUTH

Have you ever put something weird in your body?

 **OR**

As i try my best to not get wet/hard, for 5 minutes beg me to make out with you the sexiest way you know how as i resist.

DARE

TRUTH

What's something sexual i do that you like but didn't expect?

 **OR**

Kiss me as if it's the first time you've just realized you love me.

DARE

TRUTH

What's the dirtiest name you've ever called someone during sex?

 **OR**

Let me watch you masturbate to orgasm.

DARE

TRUTH

Have you ever fantasized about having a sexual experience with someone of the gender/sex you don't normally have sex with? Describe it.

 **OR**

Blindfold me and kiss and tease your favorite parts of my body for 5 minutes.

DARE

TRUTH

What sexual outfit on yourself and a partner most turns you on?

 **OR**

Guide my hand around your body for 10 minutes and show me how it gets turned on - your sensitive areas, the pressure you like, the types of touch (nails, strokes, taps etc etc)

NO WORDS ALLOWED.

DARE

TRUTH

Describe in detail, if i were to tie you up what would you want me to do to you?

 **OR**

Role play as a authority figure for 10 minutes (cop, doctor or teacher) and dominate me in a seductive way.

DARE

TRUTH

Tell me a sexual secret you have.

 **OR**

Let me spank you (i get to choose if you wear underwear or not) and count up to 10 as i spank you.

DARE

TRUTH

What's the bravest sexual thing you've ever done?

 **OR**

Give me a massage for 10 minutes without using your hands.

DARE

TRUTH

Describe what an erotic threesome would be like for you.

 **OR**

This week write me a short erotic story imagining us in a fantasy scenario that turns you on and describe the sex we'd have in lots of detail.

(Don't show me, post it to me so i receive it by next week).

DARE

TRUTH

What's the grossest thing you've ever done sexually?

 **OR**

Call a friend for a quick conversation and without telling them we're playing this game tell them how much i turn you on.

DARE

TRUTH

What do you think is the sexiest thing about you?

 **OR**

When we next travel i get to choose one new sexual thing we haven't done before for us to try.

DARE

TRUTH

What part of your body (that's not sexual) turns you on the most when I touch it?

 **OR**

Go put on my underwear and come back wearing nothing else.

DARE

TRUTH

What's the most embarrassing sexual experience you've ever had?

 **OR**

Online, order us a really kinky sex toy right now.

DARE

TRUTH

What's your darkest sexual fantasy?

 **OR**

Go to a beginners tantric sex class with me (online or in person) within the next 3 months.

DARE

TRUTH

If you were to get a tattoo by your genitals what would you pick?

 **OR**

Let me tease and play with your nipples for 10 minutes.

DARE

TRUTH

Would you rather watch someone have sex or be watched?

 **OR**

Go down on me for as long as i want.

DARE

TRUTH

If you could cast a sex spell over anyone you want to have sex with you (and they'd have a great time too), who would you pick?

 **OR**

Write me a sex- on-request coupon i can use whenever i want.

DARE

TRUTH

Would you ever have sex
with a robot?

 **OR**

Pick an erotic movie for us to
watch together next
weekend.

DARE

TRUTH

What sexual position would you like to try/do more of but have little confidence right now?

 **OR**

Play strip poker with me this month.

DARE

TRUTH

Have you ever had sex
whilst on drugs?

 **OR**

Let me tease you with
something hot for 5 minutes.

DARE

TRUTH

Tell me the dirtiest sex fantasy you've ever had with either a religious theme or school setting theme to it.

 **OR**

Get on your knees in front of me, stare into my eyes and describe the dirtiest fantasy you've ever had of us.

DARE

TRUTH

If you were to have sex in virtual reality what avatar would you pick?

 **OR**

Give me permission to do anything i want to do to you sexually for 10 minutes (as long as it's not degrading or painful - in a way you don't like).

DARE

TRUTH

Who do you think is better
at sex, me or you?

 **OR**

Pick a form of transport and time
you feel most combfortable
where i can (secretly) grope you
and get you really wet/hard for
up to 10 minutes. (You get to
decide if you want to come or
not).

DARE

TRUTH

Do romantic gestures turn you on more or kinky sexual gestures?

 **OR**

Feed me a desert in the most seductive way you can think of.

DARE

TRUTH

If you could experience what it's like to have sex in the body of someone else the same sex as you or the body of someone the opposite sex as you, which would you pick?

 **OR**

Give me a foot massage.

DARE

TRUTH

If you had to kiss someone from our friendship group who would it be?

 **OR**

Role-play how you would start the interaction leading to sex (from when i walk through the door) if i've hired you as a high class escort for one night and am a big tipper (and you secretly genuinely really find me attractive). **DARE**

TRUTH

What's currently the top 3 on your sexual bucket list?

 **OR**

Whisper in my ear a sexy nickname you've wanted to try calling me but have been to embarrassed to try.

DARE

TRUTH

Who is your guilty ugly-sexy crush?

 **OR**

Let me stare into your eyes as i make you cum by giving you a hand job/finger you.

DARE

TRUTH

What's the least sexy thing anyone's ever said to you (whilst trying to be sexy)?

 **OR**

Get naked and let me admire and play with your body for 7 minutes.

DARE

TRUTH

If you were the opposite sex for a day what is the first thing you'd do sexually?

 **OR**

Describe a sex fantasy you've had using either a British or French accent.

DARE

TRUTH

Have you ever done
anything sexually that you
feel guilty about?

 **OR**

Let me do a sexual act to
you on/against any surface
in this residence right now.

DARE

TRUTH

If you could only experience one sexual act from a partner for the rest of your life, what would you choose?

 **OR**

Next month, one evening surprise me when i come home and be in bed naked ready to have sex with me.

DARE

TRUTH

What sexual position used to really turn you on but now doesn't so much anymore?

 **OR**

Let me choose how you style your pubic hair for the next month - from bare to all there, no holds bard.

DARE

TRUTH

What do you fantasize about most regularly to make yourself cum?

 **OR**

Let me talk dirty to you for 7 minutes. If you get more hard/wet then you already are then i get to spank you for being disobedient.

DARE

TRUTH

If you were single would you sleep with someone whose just turned 'legal" if you felt you had a connection?

 **OR**

Be my sex slave for one night next month.

DARE

TRUTH

If you could double the amount in your bank account or double the amount of sex you have, which would you pick?

 **OR**

Have sex with me in a car, or garden or with the curtains open in our bedroom this month.

DARE

TRUTH

What's your biggest fear sexually?

 **OR**

Using a marker pen draw arrows on your body where you most like to be touched and write a word to describe the feeling you get at each spot.

DARE

TRUTH

Have you ever masturbated thinking of me? Describe it.

 **OR**

Use any sex toy you like on yourself for the next 2 minutes.

DARE

TRUTH

Is there anything that turns
you on that you resent?

 **OR**

Close your eyes, scroll
through your contacts list
and describe a (fantasy)
sexual act you'd like to do
to that person.

DARE

TRUTH

What sexual position do you think is my favorite?

 **OR**

Let's go to a bar or nightclub and let me grind you on the dance floor or watch as you grind with someone else.

(I get to choose).

DARE

TRUTH

Would you ever take part in an orgy?

 **OR**

Meet me at my workplace next week and in front of everyone make if clear how much you desire me and do a big PDA (public display of affection)

DARE

TRUTH

How many people have you
kissed in your life?

 **OR**

Let me tease you with
something hot for 5 minutes.

DARE

TRUTH

Is there anything about anal
play that turns you on?
Describe it.

 **OR**

Whisper in my ear
something sexual you've
always wanted to see me
do.

DARE

TRUTH

What most turns you on about the body of the sex/gender you're attracted to?

 **OR**

Pour a bowl of milk and place it in front of me on the ground. Crawl towards it on all fours and lick it up seductively.

DARE

TRUTH

What one sexual experience do you think about most often?

 **OR**

Let's try to have sex in a position you've always thought is "ridiculous" and discover what's the attraction to it.

DARE

TRUTH

Finish this sentence in 30 seconds starting NOW;

Sexually i wish...

 **OR**

Describe a dirty wedding day sex fantasy that turns you on.

DARE

TRUTH

If you could choose, how would you have liked us to have first met?

 **OR**

Turn out the lights and try to turn me on using only sounds.

DARE

TRUTH

Would it turn you on to see me making out with someone of the gender i am not normally attracted to?

 **OR**

Next time our friends visit dress more sexual and be more flirty with me then you've ever been in front of them before.

DARE

TRUTH

If you were a porn star, what kind of scenes would you like to be known for? and what porn name would you pick?

 **OR**

Do 1 shot if you've slept with up to 10 people.

Do 2 shots if you've slept with up to 20 people.

And so on...

(Or if you don't drink, dance sensually to a song each time for me).

DARE

TRUTH

If you had to have sex with one animal what animal would you choose?

 **OR**

Let me try some erotic pain/ pleasure with your nipples (light pegging/pinching and then soothing play) for 5 minutes.

DARE

TRUTH

Finish this sentence in 30 seconds;

The idea of polyamory makes me feel...

 **OR**

Slather yourself in oil whilst naked. I get to choose what happens next for 7 minutes.

DARE

TRUTH

What fictional character have you most had sexual fantasies about?

 **OR**

Plan a date night where we pretend we don't know each other and you try to seduce me, leading to us having sex.

DARE

TRUTH

Describe how you would like the sex to have gone if we lost our virginity to each other? (being the same ages we each were in real life)

 **OR**

Convince me to buy you as a sex slave - by offering me services that you have to actually do right now.

DARE

TRUTH

What can i do on a regular basis that will get you in the mood for sex?

 **OR**

Use your tongue to spell out your name on any part of my body.

DARE

TRUTH

If you could have an affair (but have the power to turn back time - but remember what you did) would you consider that cheating? and would you do it?

 **OR**

Let me select an entire outfit for you to wear when we go on a date next month.

DARE

TRUTH

When do you feel most
sexiest?

 **OR**

Suck or kiss a part of my
body you never normally
do.

DARE

TRUTH

If you had to choose between only oral sex or penetrative sex for the rest of your life, which one would you choose?

 **OR**

Use a piece of fruit to demonstrate your oral sex skills.

DARE

TRUTH

If you had the power to give or receive unlimited orgasms, what would you pick?

 **OR**

Become my sexual serving platter next week. Let me dine on you naked as food is served on your naked body.

DARE

TRUTH

Describe our sex life in three words.

 **OR**

One night this month let's role-play as if you don't want to have sex and i forcibly seduce you in some way. I decide on the storyline.

(Of course let's make sure actual consent is given beforehand via a 'safe word' we decide on now.)

DARE

TRUTH

What's your favorite part of foreplay?

 **OR**

Be topless for the next 7 minutes.

DARE

TRUTH

If we were to have a threesome would you pick another man or woman to join us?

 **OR**

Give me a lap dance.

DARE

TRUTH

What sex act disgusts you
the most?

 **OR**

Do whatever i say for 1 hour
tomorrow.

DARE

TRUTH

What's the biggest lie you've told in order to get someone else to be attracted to you?

 **OR**

I'm going on a porn site and have a 5 minute deadline to find a clip of a scene that we will do together right now.

DARE

TRUTH

What's the meanest thought you've had about someone else sexually?

 **OR**

Describe your genitalia as a product as if you were selling it for 3 minutes.

DARE

TRUTH

What's the sexiest thing anyone's ever said to you?

 **OR**

Kiss, nuzzle, tease and bite my neck and ear lobes for 10 minutes.

DARE

TRUTH

During your marriage would you like to both have permission to "stray" once?

 **OR**

Let me put a blindfold on you and you must kiss whatever body part I put in front of your mouth.

DARE

TRUTH

Finish this sentence in 30 seconds;

The idea of polygamy makes me feel...

 **OR**

Pick a week and i will spend the whole week pursuing you and being super flirty and seductive. You must ensure we don't have sex till the last day. If you "give in" before then, then you have to be my sex slave for everyday of the following week.

DARE

TRUTH

Would you like to go to a sex party (if you didn't have to take part and could wear a mask?)

 **OR**

Let's have a sex do-over of your most embarrassing or disappointing sexual experience...let's recreate that scenario and do it right this time.

DARE

TRUTH

What do you wish you'd known sexually at 18 years old?

 **OR**

Next month surprise me by wrapping yourself up as a present with just a bow whilst naked and offer yourself to me for the night as my new toy to play with.

DARE

TRUTH

If you found out your partner had sex with someone else would you prefer they genuinely cared about that person or it was purely sex?

 **OR**

Let me watch you masturbate.

DARE

TRUTH

What smell turns you on
sexually?

 **OR**

Sit on my lap (or vice versa if
appropriate) and let me act like i'm
selling you as a sex object to my
good business associates
demonstrating to them all the sexual
benefits of your body and how and
where you like to get turned on and
eventually show them how you
orgasm. **DARE**

TRUTH

If you could have 3 sexual
wishes what would they be?

 **OR**

Kiss and lick my entire body
for 15 minutes.

DARE

TRUTH

What texture turns you on
the most sexually?

 **OR**

Let's go out to dinner and
you wear no panties/no
briefs and let me play with
you secretly whilst we're out.

DARE

TRUTH

Describe what my cum tastes like.

 **OR**

Get something from the fridge and eat it as seductively as possible as if you are savouring eating a piece of me.

DARE

TRUTH

What are you most insecure
about sexually?

 **OR**

Let me watch you shower -
make it a sexy one!

DARE

TRUTH

What's something you've fantasized about but are certain you would never want to experience in real life?

 **OR**

Let's both wear blindfolds and for 15 minutes play and explore each others bodies.

DARE

TRUTH

Would you rather have sex with someone 20 years younger or older?

 **OR**

Make a sex tape with me (i get to decide the content) and then let's watch it once together afterwards and then we have to delete it.

DARE

Hope you had lots of fun!

Now go have some more...

Printed in Great Britain
by Amazon

62755543R00061